Tiny's Big Discovery

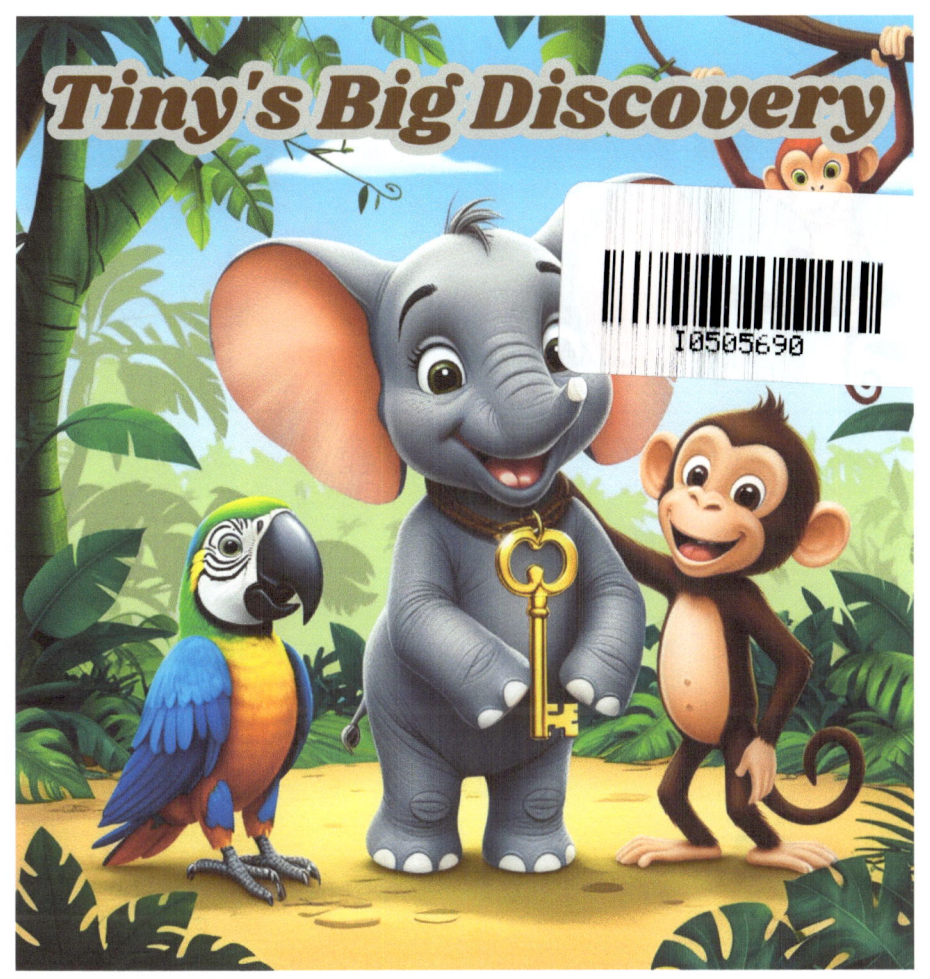

Tiny the Elephant was the smallest in the jungle. One sunny day, he found a shiny, golden key buried beneath some leaves.

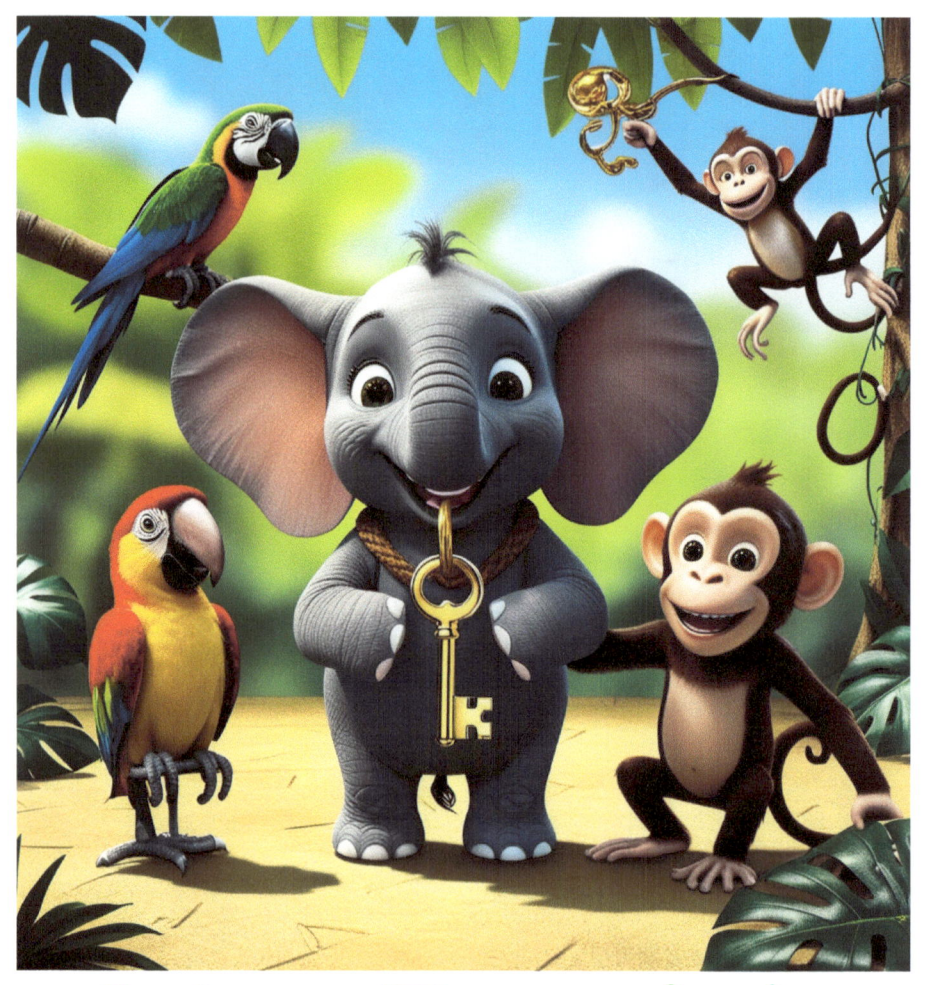

Curious, Tiny took the
key to his best friends:
Ruby the Parrot and Max
the Monkey. They
wondered what it could
unlock.

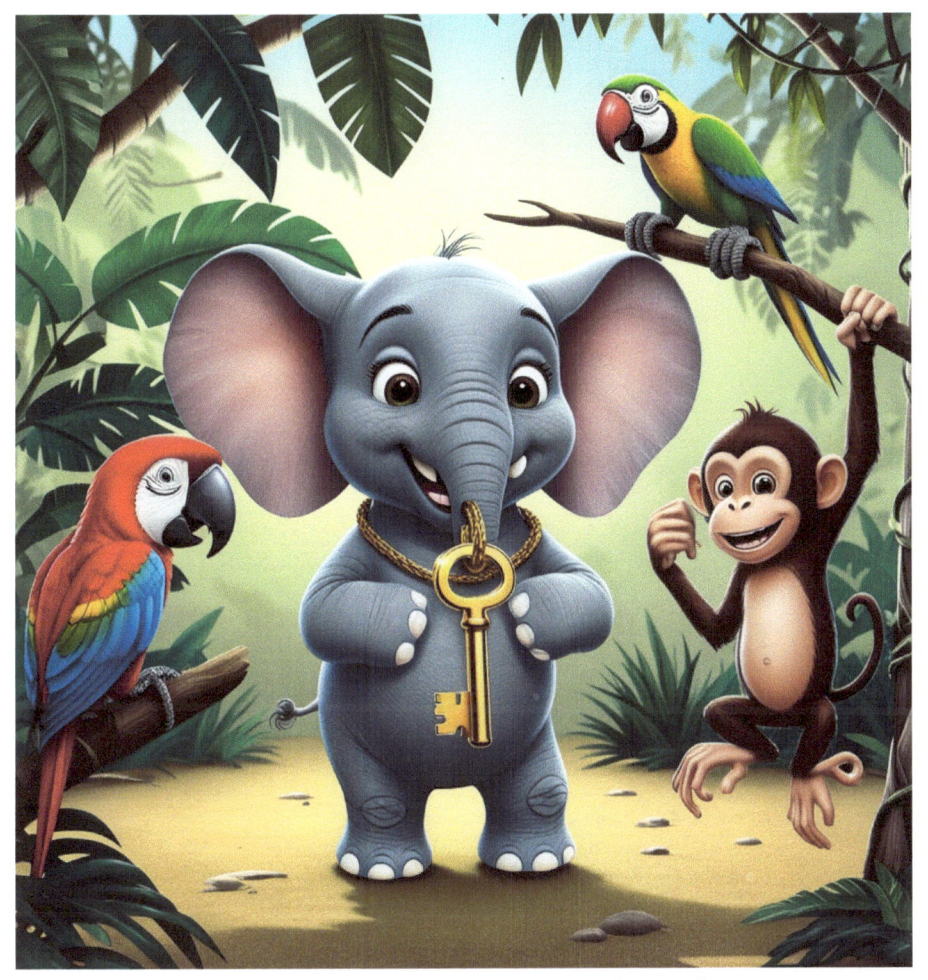

Max suggested they explore the jungle to find the matching lock. Tiny, excited by the idea, eagerly agreed to the adventure.

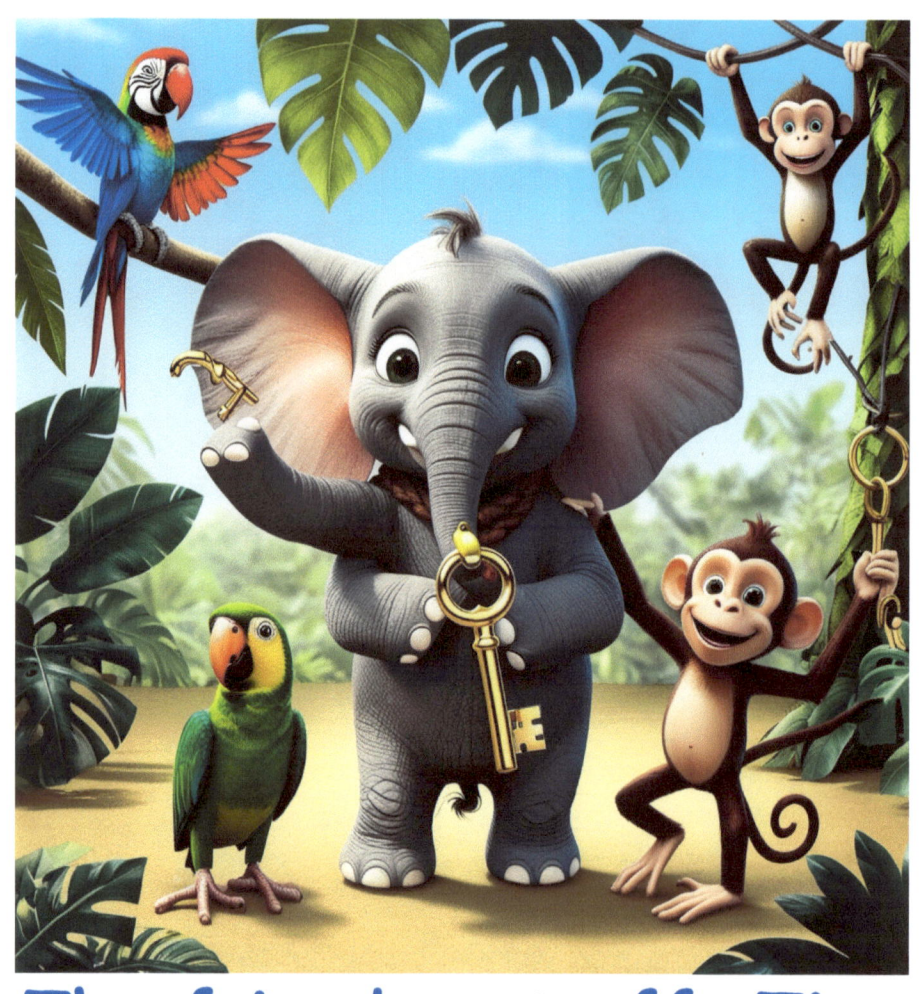

The friends set off, Tiny leading the way with the key around his neck. Their hearts were full of excitement and curiosity.

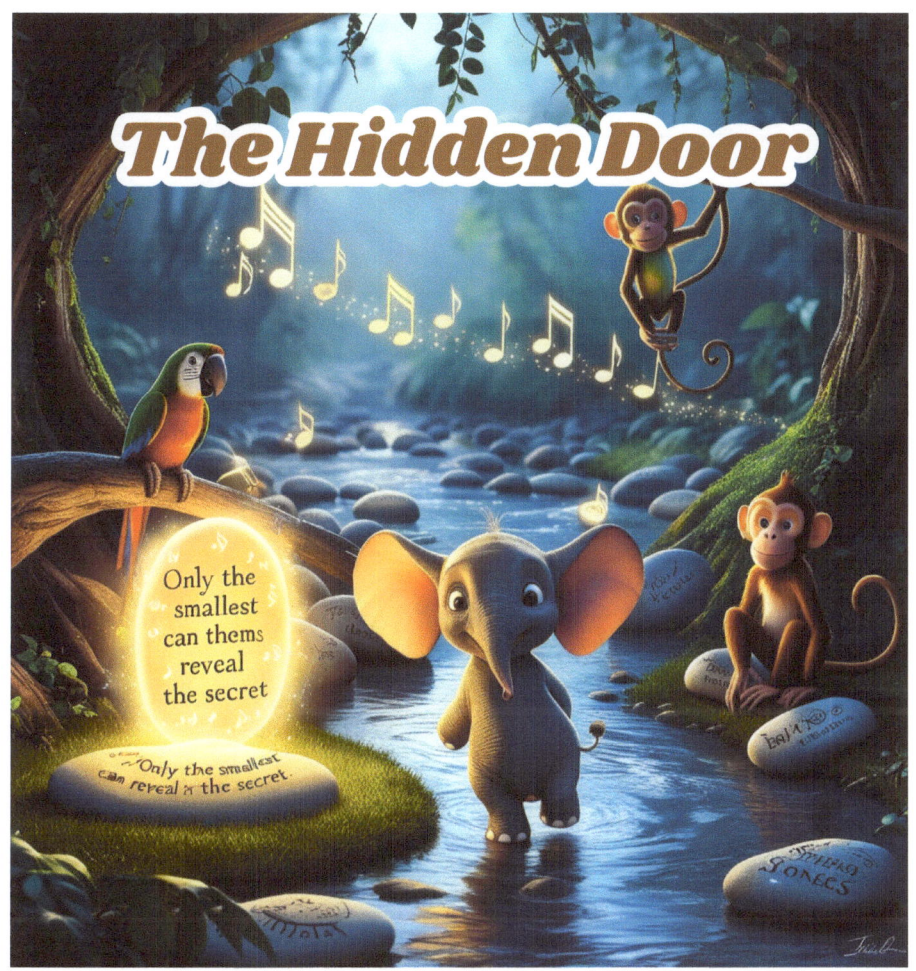

As they wandered, Tiny spotted a peculiar tree with a hidden door. The door was tiny, just like Tiny. Could this be it?

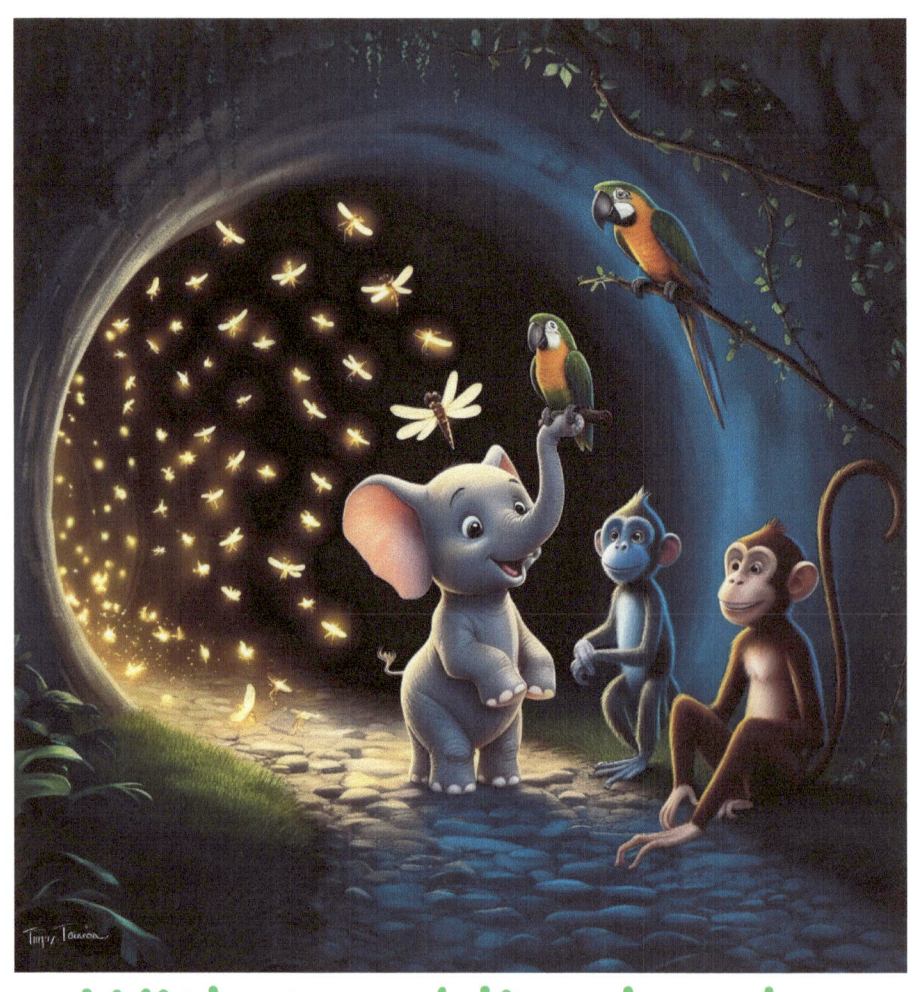

With trembling hands, Tiny inserted the key into the lock. It fit perfectly! The door creaked open to reveal a dark tunnel.

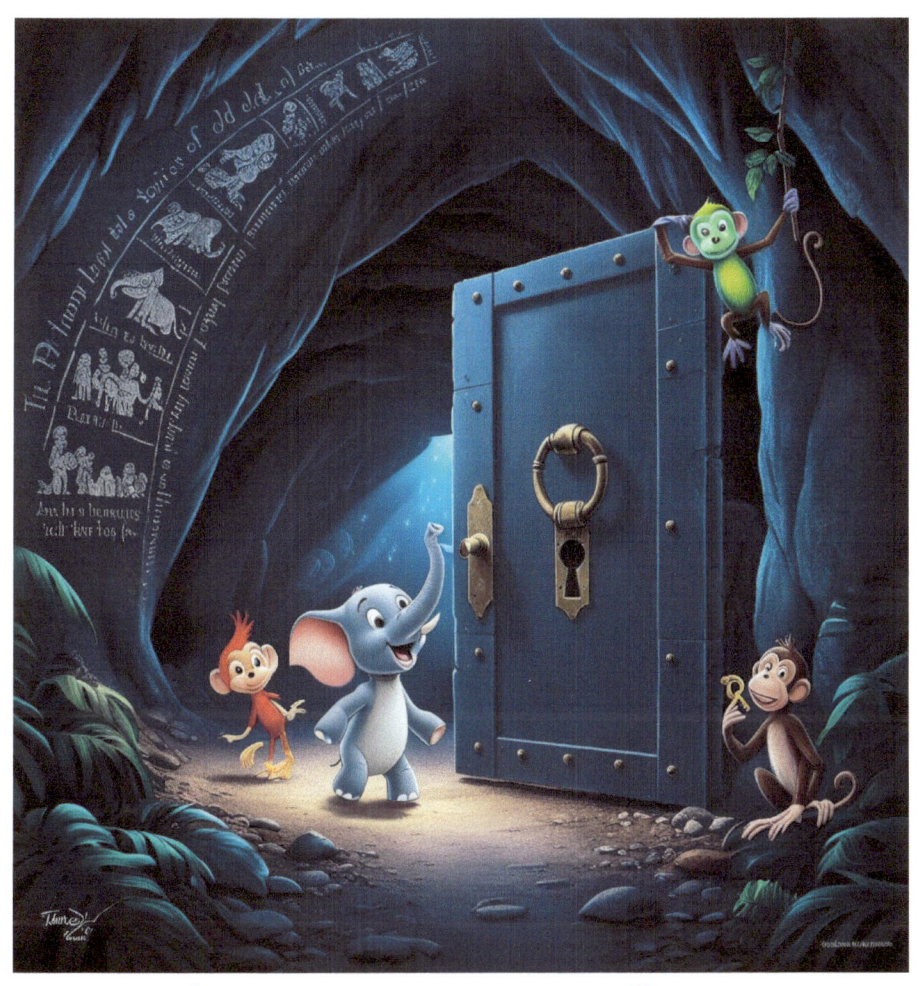

Ruby, Max, and Tiny bravely stepped inside. Glowing crystals lit their path, casting magical light. Tiny felt a surge of adventure.

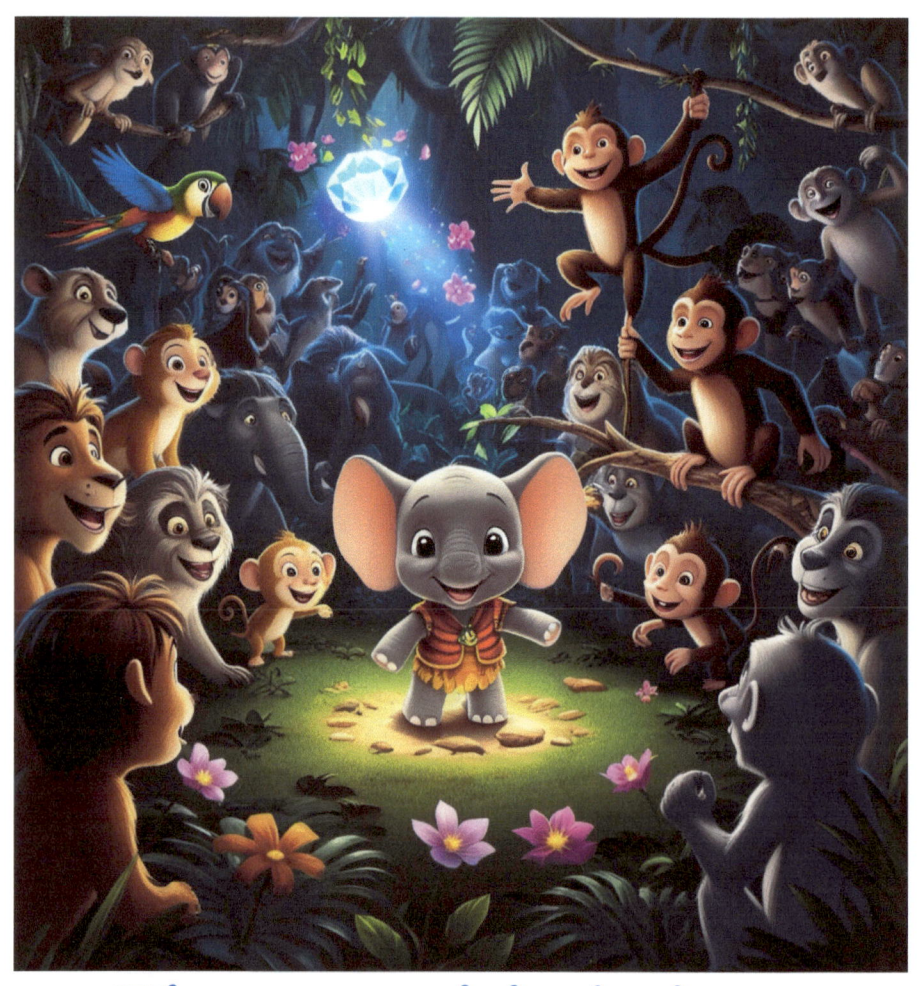

The tunnel led them
deeper into the jungle,
uncovering paths no one
had ever seen. Tiny's
small size made him
perfect for this quest.

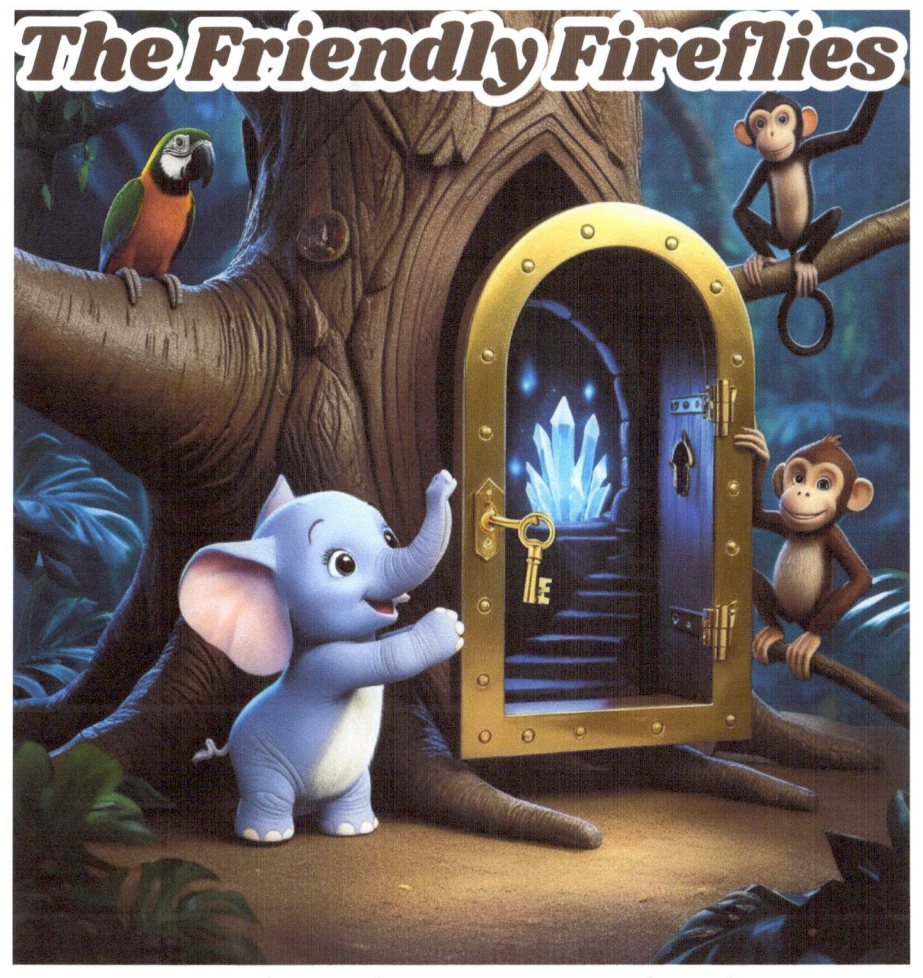

The Friendly Fireflies

In the heart of the tunnel, they met a swarm of fireflies. The fireflies danced around them, lighting up the entire tunnel.

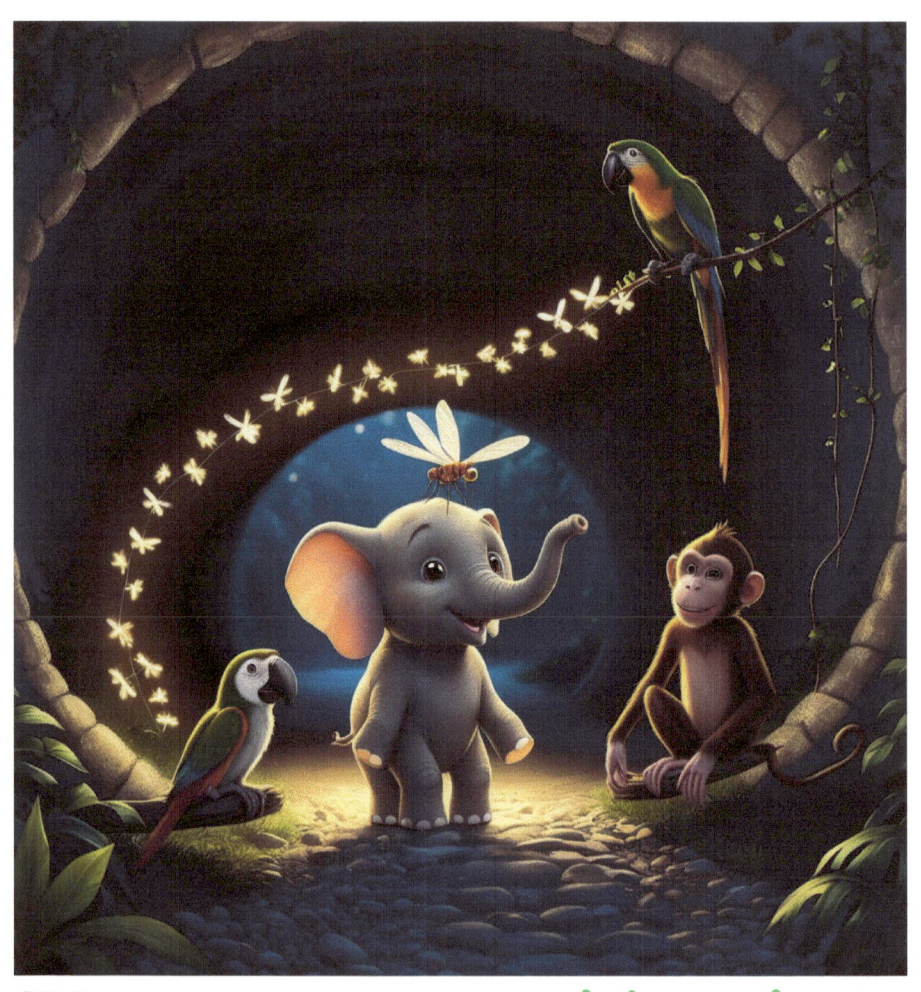

Tiny was amazed by their beauty. One firefly landed on his trunk, whispering directions to the next part of their journey.

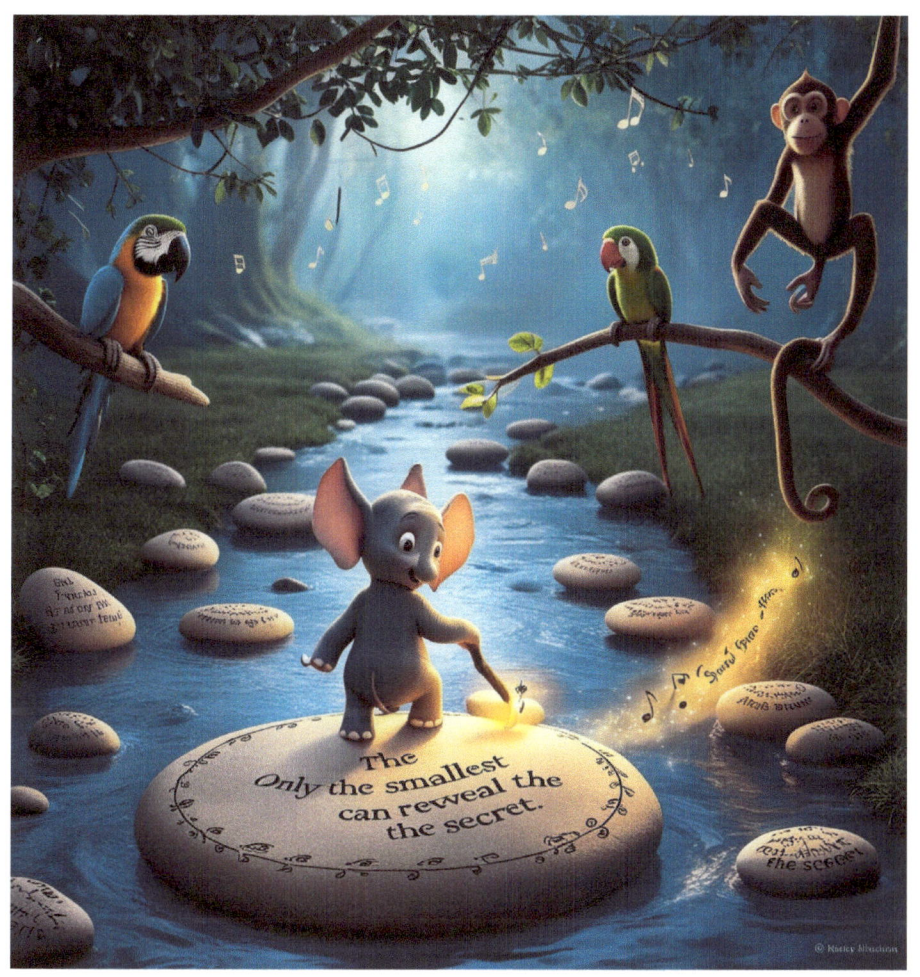

The fireflies guided them to a hidden underground river. Tiny felt grateful for their help. His small size made him their favorite.

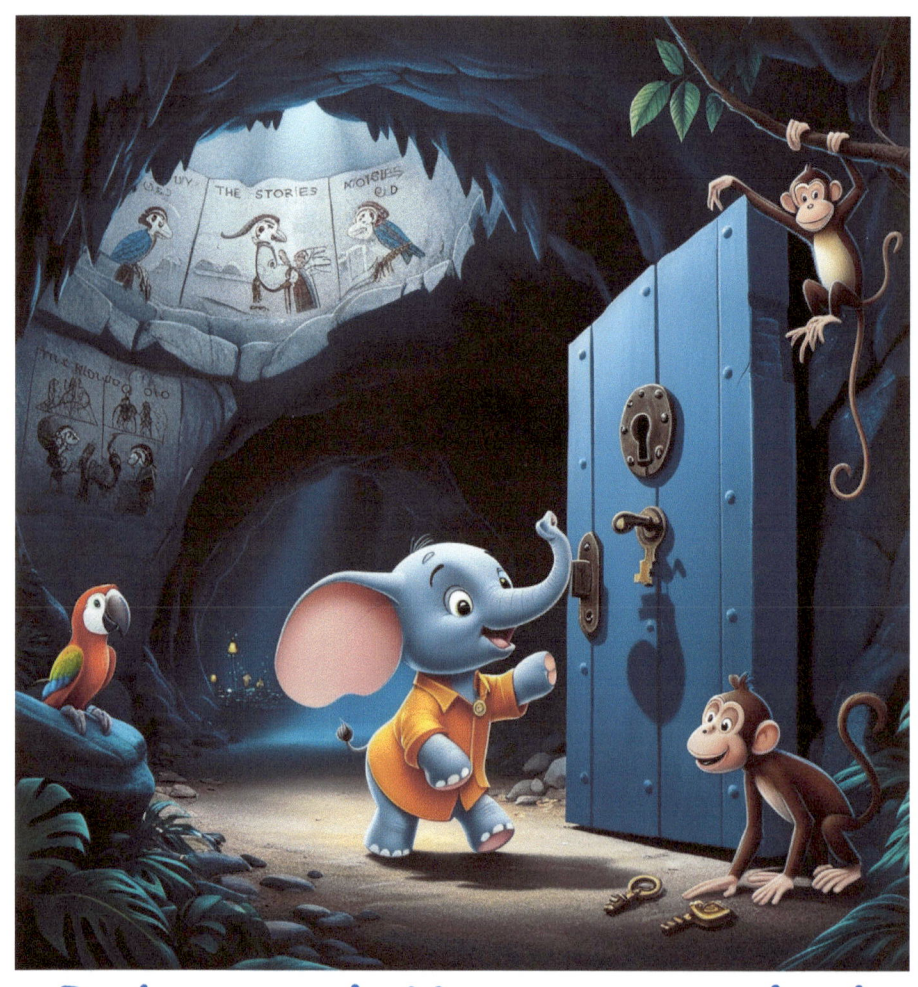

Ruby and Max marveled
at the sight. They knew
Tiny's bravery and small
size had led them to this
magical moment.

The Singing Stones

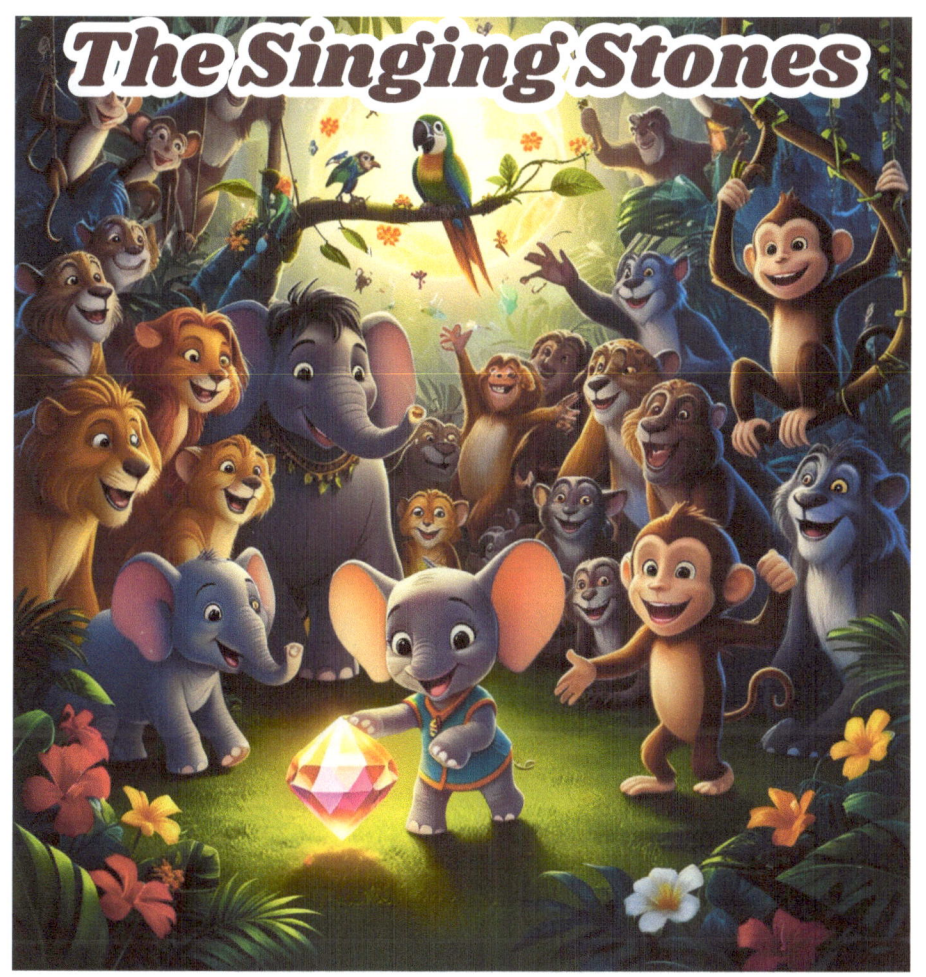

As they followed the river, they heard a beautiful melody. Tiny's ears perked up, leading them to a circle of singing stones.

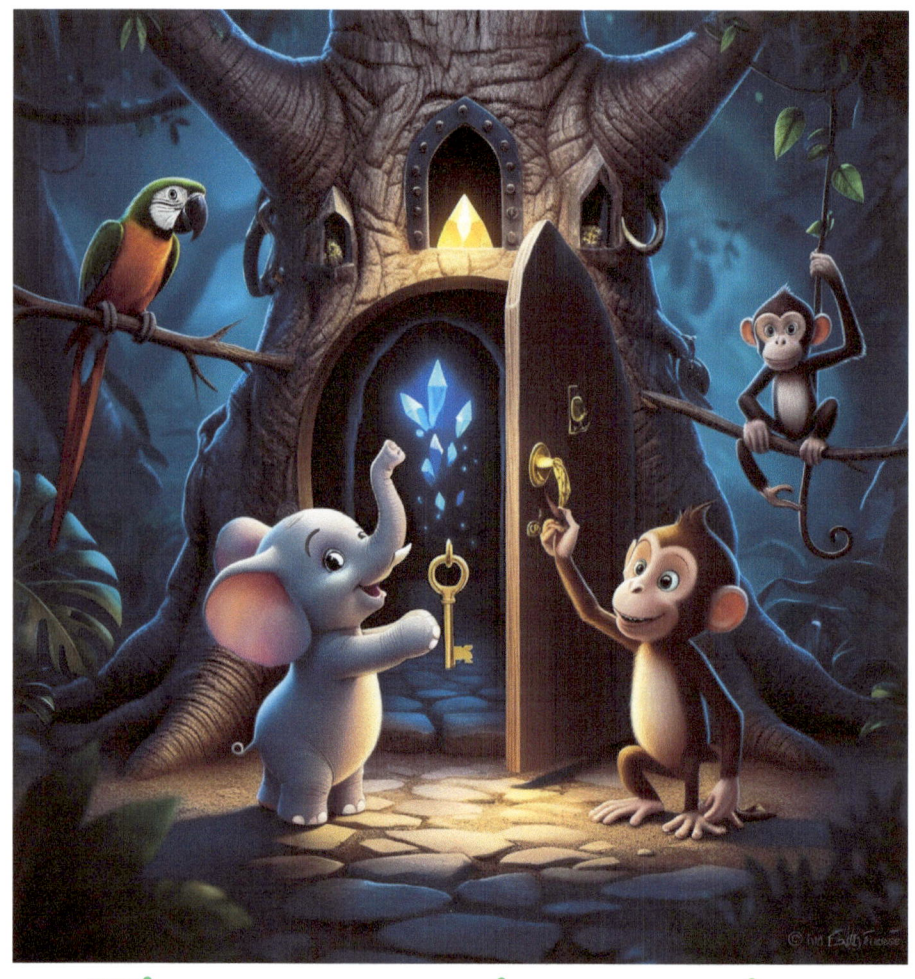

The stones hummed a gentle tune. Tiny, Ruby, and Max listened, feeling the music fill their hearts. The stones seemed alive.

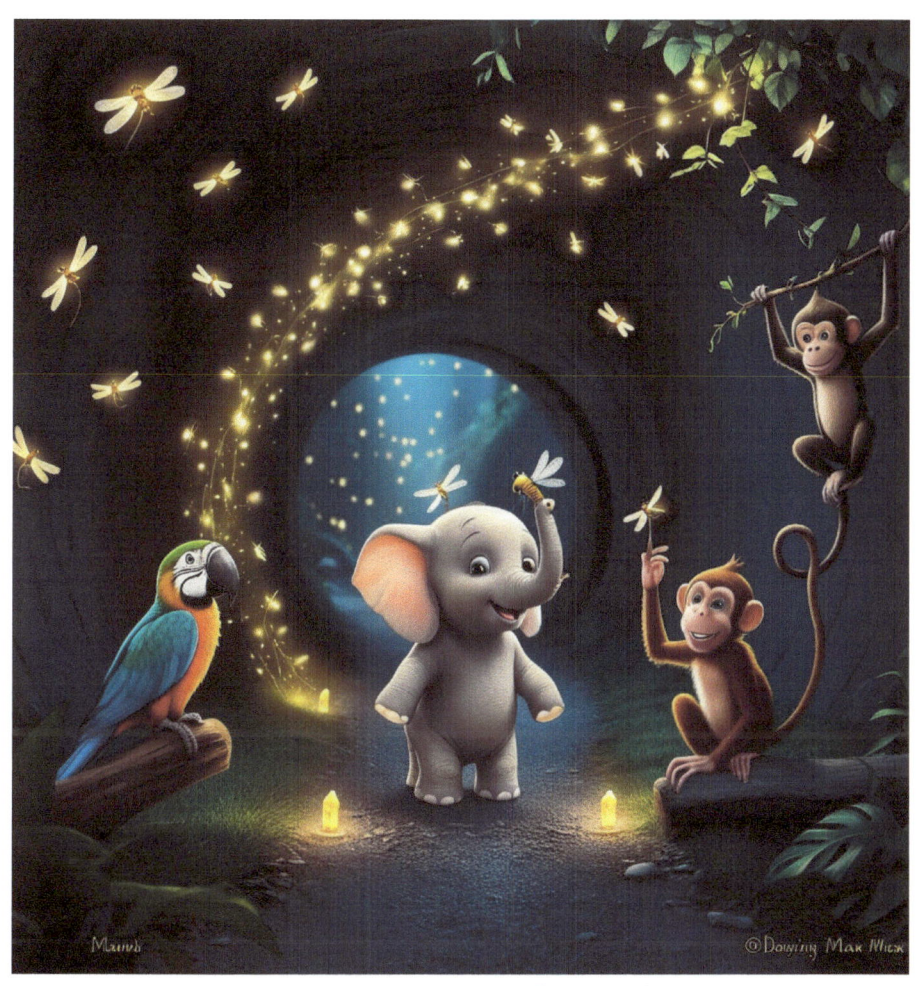

One stone had an engraving: "Only the smallest can reveal the secret." Tiny stepped forward, touching the stone with his trunk.

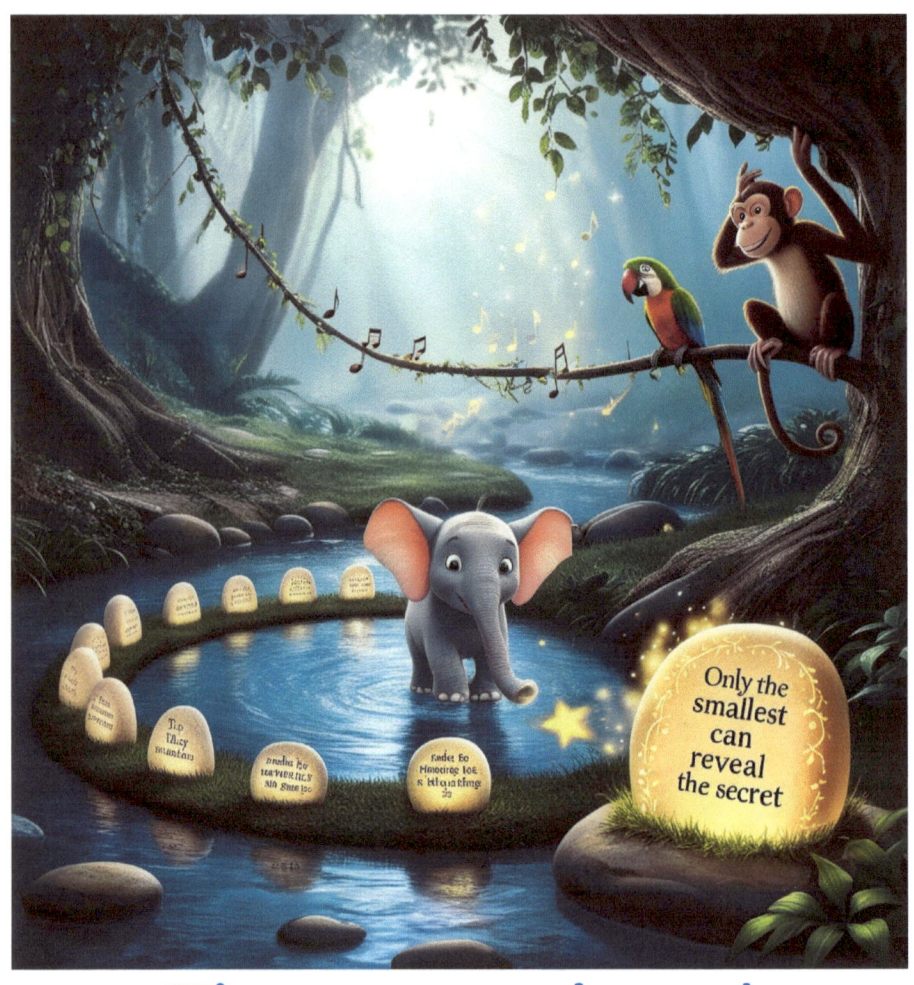

The stone glowed brightly, revealing a hidden message. Tiny read it aloud, "Follow the music to find the heart of the treasure

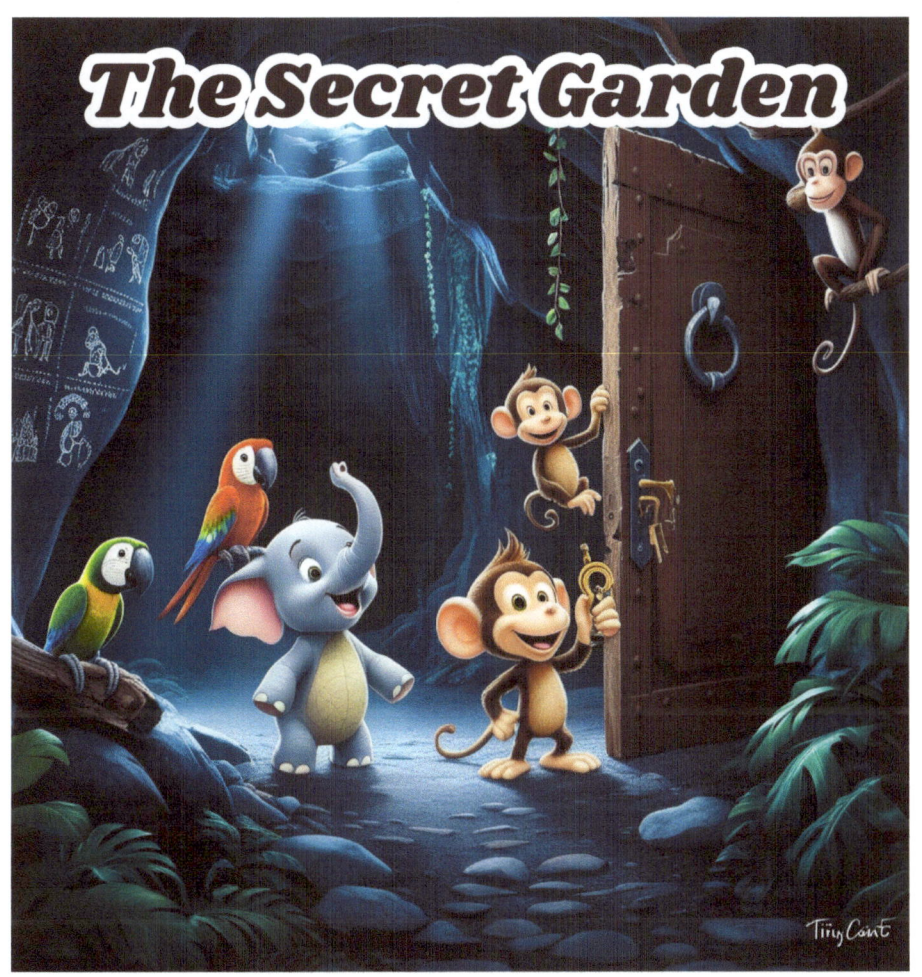

The music led them to a secret garden, hidden deep within the jungle. The garden was filled with colorful flowers and sparkling streams.

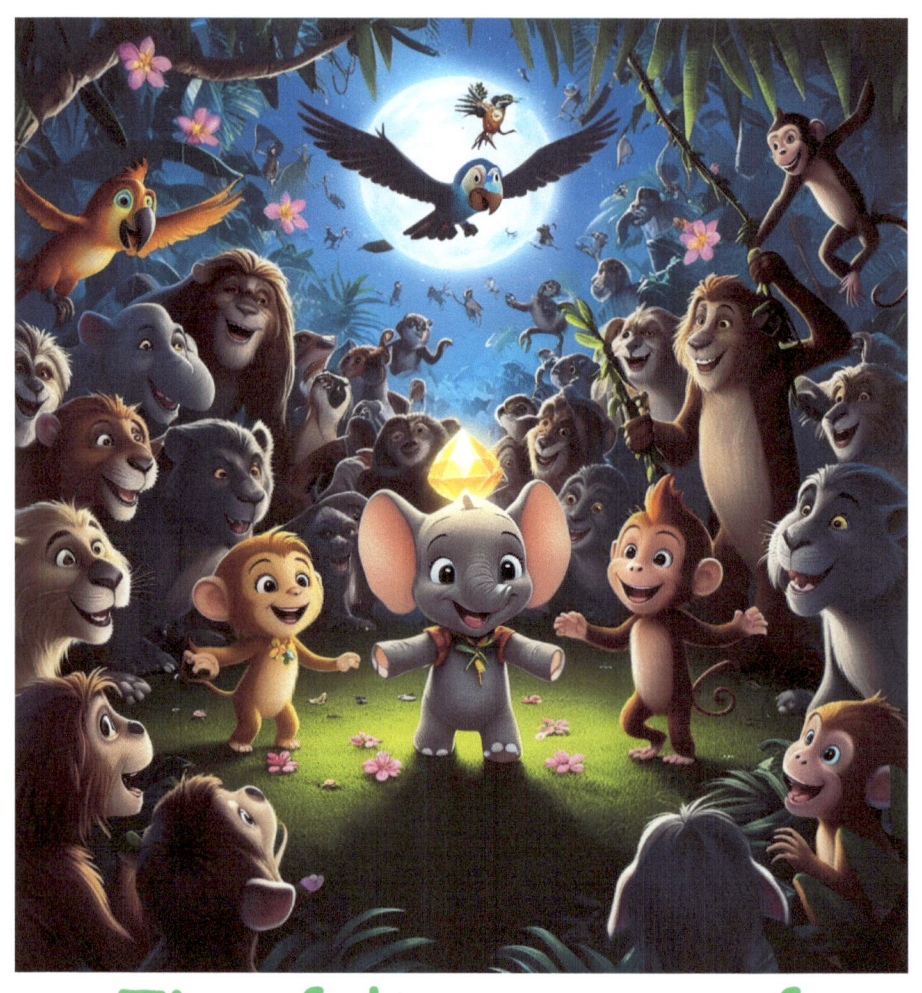

Tiny felt a sense of wonder. Ruby and Max were equally enchanted. In the center, they found a small, ornate chest.

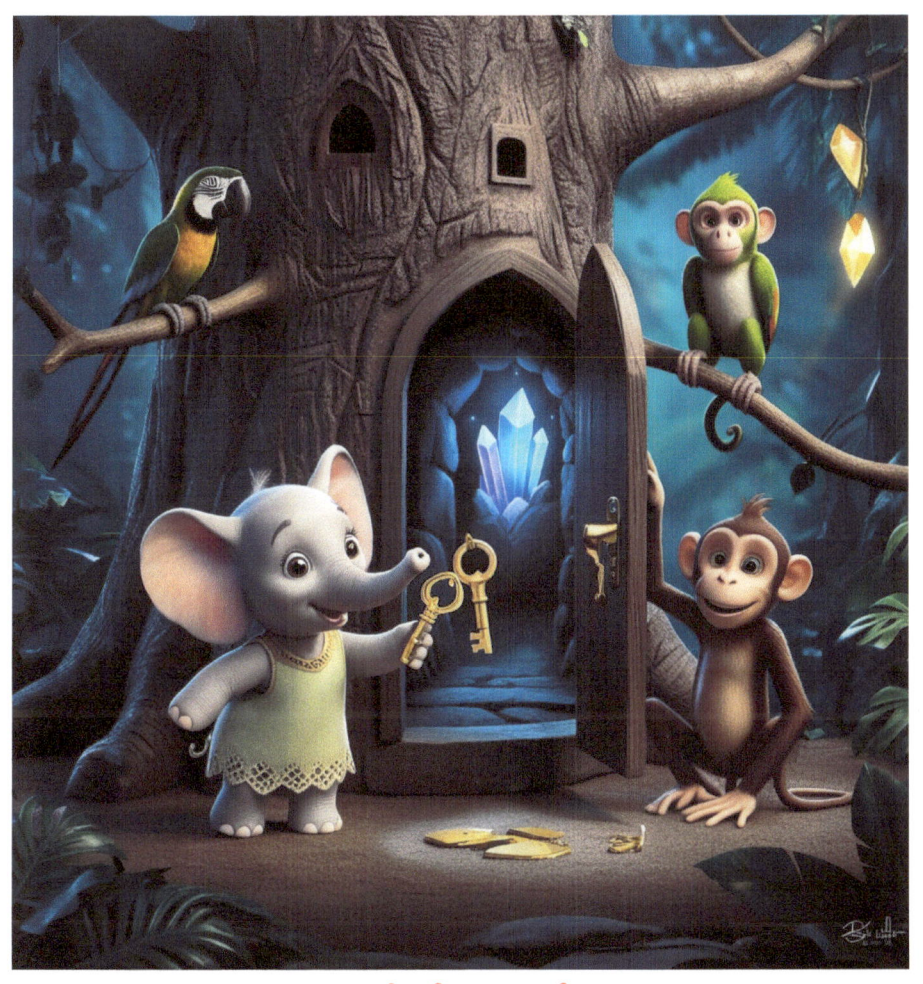

Tiny used his key once more, opening the chest. Inside was a glowing gem, radiating warmth and light. It was breathtaking.

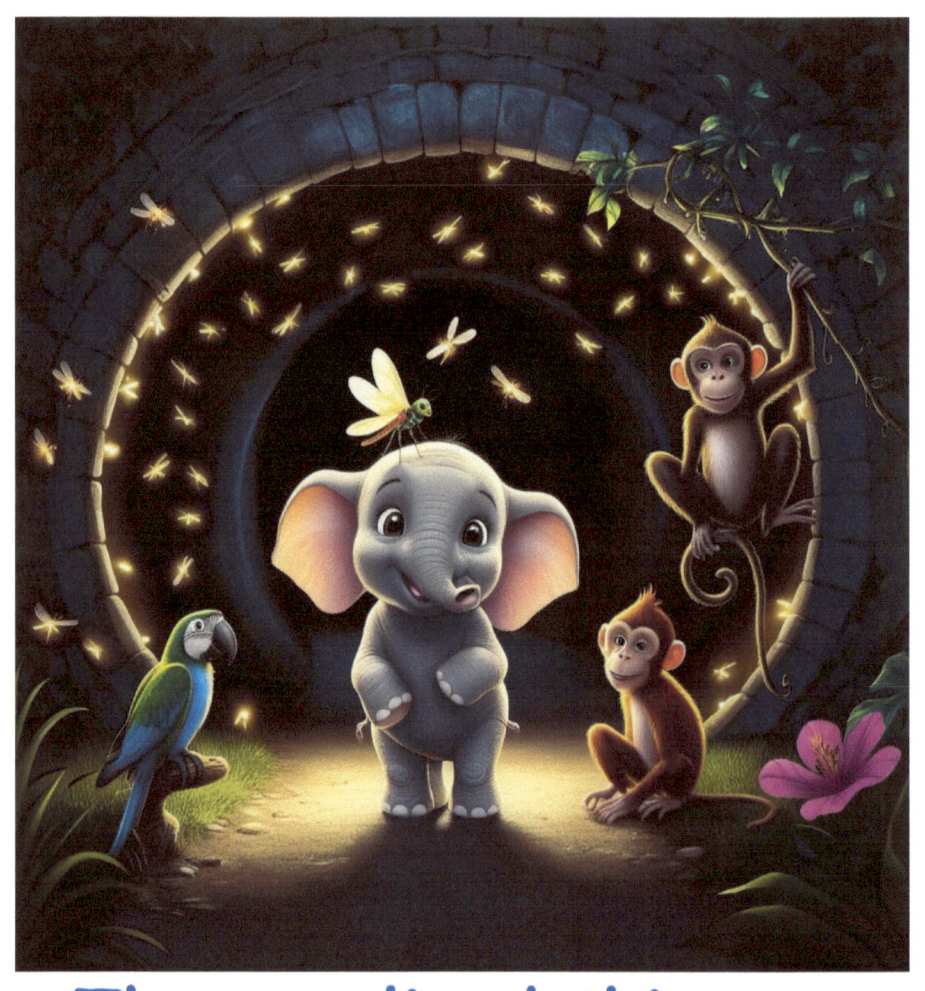

They realized this was the heart of the treasure. The gem's magic would bring joy and harmony to the entire jungle.

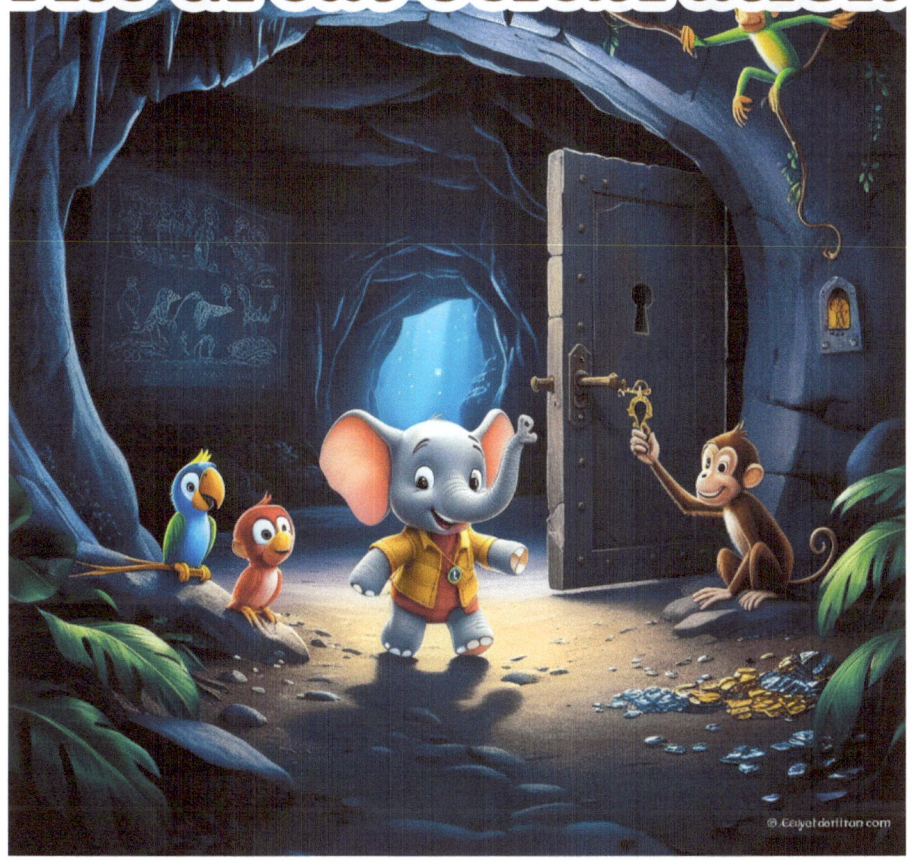

The Great Celebration

Tiny, Ruby, and Max returned home with the gem. The jungle animals gathered, curious about their discovery. Tiny shared their adventure

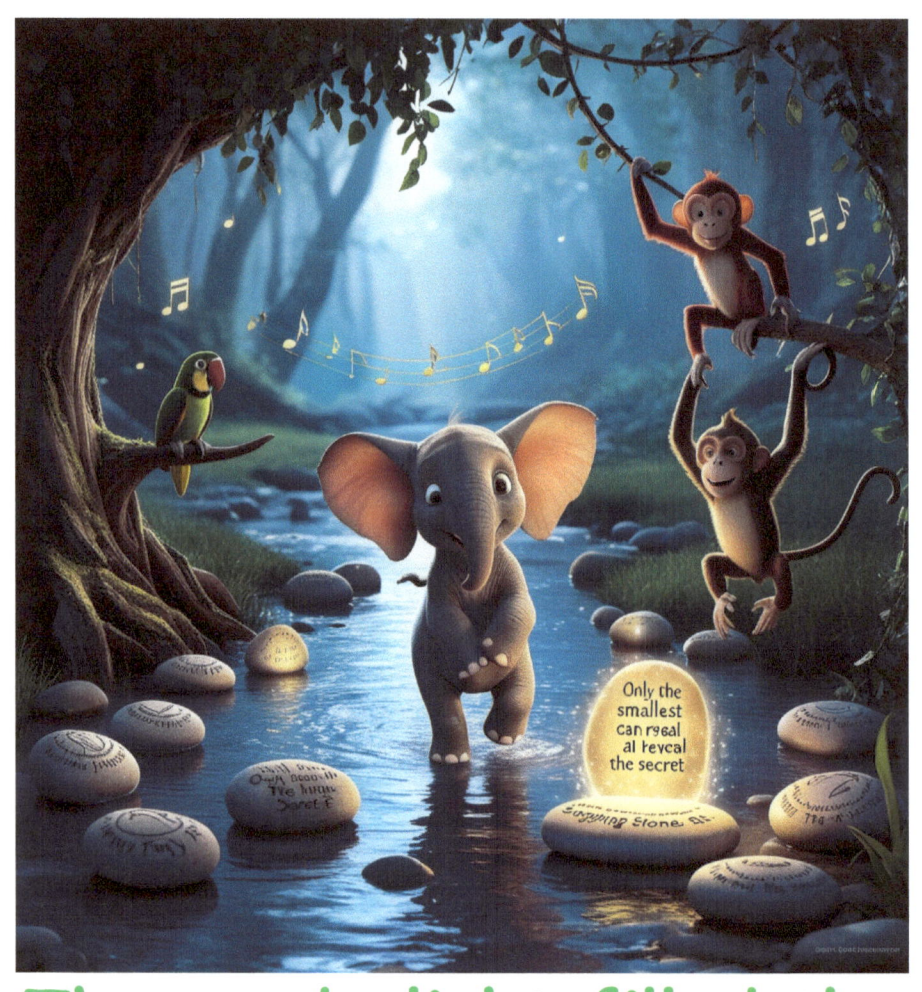

The gem's light filled the jungle, making flowers bloom and animals sing. Tiny's small size had unlocked a great treasure for all.

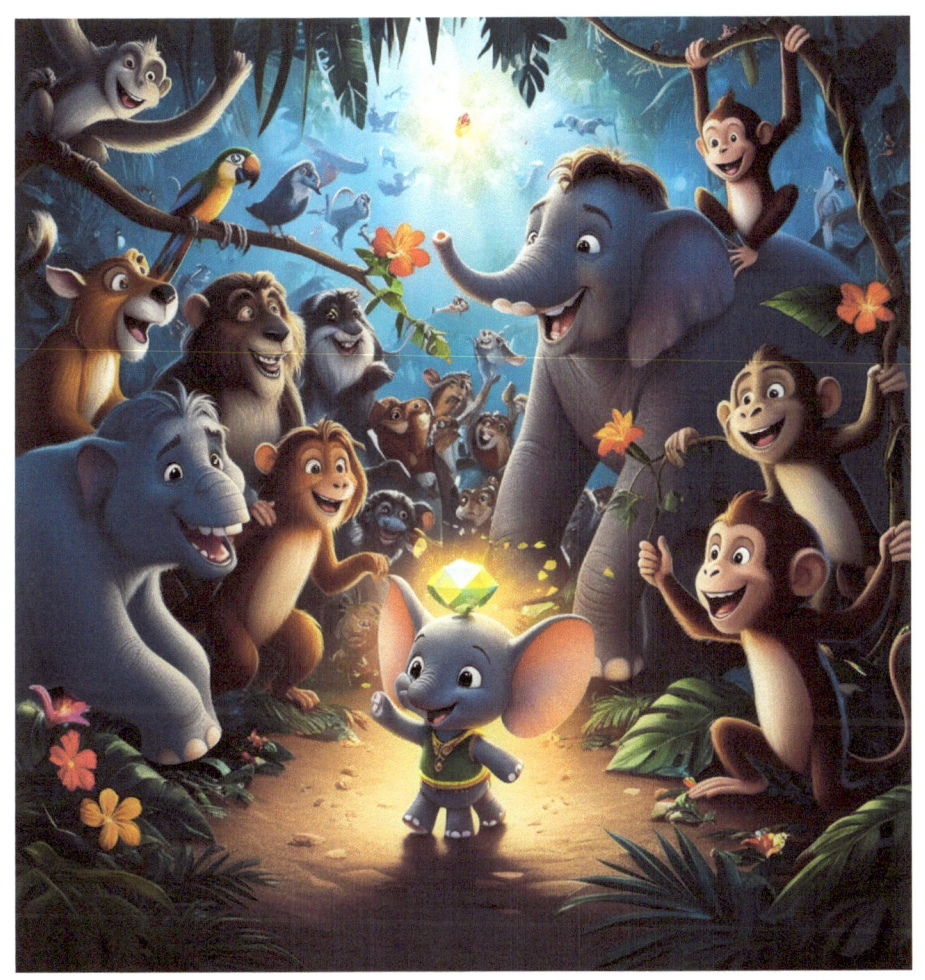

The jungle celebrated Tiny's bravery and kindness. He had shown that even the smallest could achieve great things. Tiny felt proud.

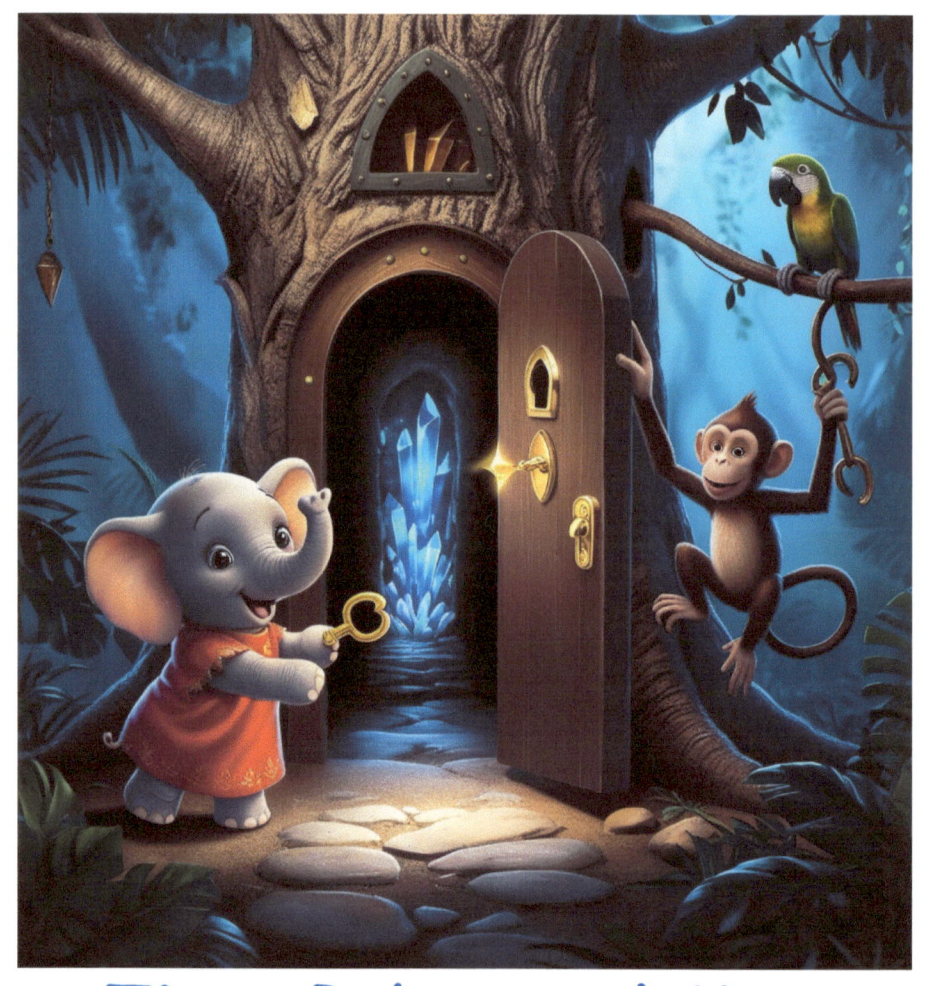

Tiny, Ruby, and Max knew many adventures awaited. With friends by his side and a brave heart, Tiny was ready for anything!